This journal belongs to

_____

_____

DATE BEGUN

_____

DATE ENDED

The

PRAYER

of

JABEZ

JOURNAL

Based on *The Prayer of Jabez*
by Bruce Wilkinson

Multnomah Publishers® *Sisters, Oregon*

THE PRAYER OF JABEZ JOURNAL
published by Multnomah Publishers, Inc.
© 2001 by Bruce Wilkinson

International Standard Book Number: 1-57673-860-4

Cover design by David Carlson
Cover image by Tatsuhiko Shimada/Photonica

Scripture quotations are from:
The Holy Bible, New King James Version
© 1984 by Thomas Nelson, Inc.

Multnomah is a trademark of Multnomah Publishers, Inc.,
and is registered in the U.S. Patent and Trademark Office.
The colophon is a trademark of Multnomah Publishers, Inc.

Printed in the United States of America

For information:
MULTNOMAH PUBLISHERS, INC.
POST OFFICE BOX 1720
SISTERS, OREGON 97759

01 02 03 04 05—10 9 8 7 6 5 4 3 2 1 0

CAPTURING THE MIRACLES DAY BY DAY

Dear friend,

If you've been praying the prayer of Jabez, you've embarked on an unusual adventure with God. Because you have asked boldly, He is blessing greatly—and your life is beginning to change in ways you never thought possible.

Why miss a minute of it? *The Prayer of Jabez Journal* has been especially designed as a tool to accompany *The Prayer of Jabez Devotional,* a thirty-one-day personal journey that takes you further into the Jabez experience. Together, the Jabez journal and devotional will help you capture remarkable miracles and live them to the fullest for the rest of your life.

Use the pages of this spiritual journal to write down your urgent prayers and to record His amazing answers. As you learn to live in the power and protection of God, you'll know how to make every day count for eternity. As you trace the evidences of His Spirit at work—in your Bible readings, in your "Jabez appointments," in your dreams and goals—you'll see even more clearly the extraordinary dimensions of what God wants for you.

I promise you that the more you capture the miracles, the more you'll reach for them with all your heart!

Warmly,

Bruce Wilkinson

And Jabez called

on the God of Israel saying,

"Oh, that You would bless me indeed,

and enlarge my territory,

that Your hand would be with me,

and that You would keep me from evil,

that I may not cause pain!"

So God granted him what

he requested.

1 CHRONICLES 4:10

Begin at once; before you venture away
from this quiet moment, ask your King to take
you wholly into His service, and place all the hours
of this day quite simply at His disposal, and ask Him to
make and keep you ready to do just exactly
what He appoints. Never mind about tomorrow;
one day at a time is enough. Try it today, and see if
it is not a day of strange, almost curious
peace, so sweet that you will be only too thankful
when tomorrow comes to ask Him to take it
also.

Frances Ridley Havergal

But looking at them, Jesus said,
"With men it is impossible, but not with God;
for with God all things are possible."

MARK 10:27

Where has there ever been found a single blessing
save in the hand of Christ?
Could you wish for any, save what He gives?

GEORGE V. WIGRAM

*Jabez was blessed simply because he refused
to let any obstacle, person, or opinion
loom larger than God's nature.
And God's nature is to bless.*

THE PRAYER OF JABEZ

Prayer is God's ordained way to bring
His miracle power to bear in human need.

WESLEY L. DUEWEL

_For we do not have a High Priest who cannot
        sympathize with our weaknesses,
but was in all points tempted as we are, yet without sin.
        Let us therefore come boldly to the throne of grace,
that we may obtain mercy and find grace to help in time of need._

HEBREWS 4:15–16

_Remember, also, that God delights to
bestow blessing, but generally
as the result of earnest, believing prayer._

GEORGE MUELLER

The Lord gives His blessing when
He finds the vessel empty.

THOMAS À KEMPIS

This is the secret of all blessing—
giving the Lord the supreme place.

EDWARD DENNETT

Have thy tools ready; God will find thee work.

CHARLES KINGSLEY

Jesus is more ready to pardon than you are to sin,
more willing to supply your wants
than you are to confess them.

CHARLES SPURGEON

_O_ God and King, please expand my opportunities
and my impact in such a way
that I touch more lives for Your glory.
Let me do more for You!

THE PRAYER OF JABEZ

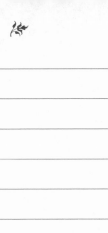

What we have done for ourselves alone dies with us.
What we have done for others and the world
remains and is immortal.

ALBERT PINE

Expect great things from God; attempt great t

W

*Think about it: How would your day unfold
        if you believed God wants your borders expanded
at all times with every person and if you were confident
        that God's powerful hand is directing you
                even as you minister?*

THE PRAYER OF JABEZ

Listen, my beloved brethren:
 Has God not chosen the poor of this world
to be rich in faith and heirs of the kingdom
 which He promised to those who love Him?

JAMES 2:5

_____

_____

_____

_____

_____

_____

_____

_____

_____

_____

_____

_____

_____

_____

_____

_____

_____

I live in the spirit of prayer;
    I pray as I walk, when I lie down, and when I rise,
and the answers are always coming.

One day in the city of New York—oh! what a day—
I cannot describe it, I seldom refer to it—
is almost too sacred an experience to name.
I can only say God revealed
Himself to me, and I had such an experience of His
love that I had to ask Him to stay His hand.
I went to preaching again. The sermons were no
different. I did not present any new ideas, yet hundreds
were converted. I would not be
placed back where I was before that blessed
experience if you were to give me all of Glasgow.

Dwight L. Moody

*The hand of God never deals but in concert
with His heart of infinite love toward us.*

JOHN DARBY

God's great plan for you will surround
you and sweep you forward into the profoundly
important and satisfying life He has waiting.

THE PRAYER OF JABEZ

*W*e can walk without fear,
    full of hope and courage and strength...waiting for the
endless good which God is always giving us as fast as
    He can get us to take it in.

GEORGE MACDONALD

Faith never yet outstripped the bounty of the Lord.

ANONYMOUS

Be still, and know that I am God.

PSALM 46:10

Four things let us ever keep in mind:
  God hears prayer, God heeds prayer,
    God answers prayer, and God delivers by prayer.

E. M. BOUNDS

_____

_____

_____

_____

_____

_____

_____

_____

_____

_____

_____

_____

_____

_____

_____

_____

In the morning prayer is the key that opens to us the
treasures of God's mercies and blessings....

AUTHOR UNKNOWN

※

_____

_____

_____

_____

_____

_____

_____

_____

_____

_____

_____

_____

_____

_____

_____

_____

_____

_____

_____

_____

Our God specializes in working through normal people
who believe in a supernormal God
who will do His work through them.

THE PRAYER OF JABEZ

We have a God who delights in impossibilities.

ANDREW MURRAY

God's work done in God's way will never lack God's supply.

$\mathcal{D}$o not lead us into temptation,
But deliver us from the evil one."

MATTHEW 6:13

You could call God's hand on you "the touch of greatness."
You do not become great;

He becomes great through you.

*E*ye has not seen, nor ear heard,
    Nor have entered into the heart of man
The things which God has prepared for those who love Him."

I CORINTHIANS 2:9

God's will is delicious. He makes no mistakes.

FRANCES RIDLEY HAVERGAL

For You, O LORD, *will bless the righteous;*
With favor You will surround him.

My prayers, my God, flow from what I am not;
I think Thy answers make me what I am.

GEORGE MACDONALD

If we knew the heart of our Father
      we would never question any of His dealings with us,
nor should we ever desire His hand lifted off us
      till we had learned all He would teach us.

EDWARD DENNETT

_____

_____

_____

_____

_____

_____

_____

_____

_____

_____

_____

_____

_____

_____

_____

_____

_____

*Prayer is the product of a humble heart,
a believing heart, and a heart renewed by grace.*

CHARLES SPURGEON

And whatever you do in word or deed,
    do all in the name of the Lord Jesus,
        giving thanks to God the Father through Him.

COLOSSIANS 3:17

I never prayed sincerely and earnestly for anything but it came at some time; no matter how distant a day, somehow, in some shape, probably the least I would have devised,

it came.

Adoniram Judson

❦

You never become truly spiritual by
sitting down and wishing to become so.
You must undertake something so great that you
cannot accomplish it unaided.

PHILLIPS BROOKS

_____

_____

_____

_____

_____

_____

_____

_____

_____

_____

_____

_____

_____

_____

_____

_____

*P*ray for great things, expect great things,
      work for great things, but above all, pray.

R. A. TORREY

To pray for larger borders is to ask for a miracle—
    it's that simple.
A miracle is an intervention by God to make something happen
    that wouldn't normally happen.

THE PRAYER OF JABEZ

❧

Watch and pray, lest you enter into temptation.
The spirit indeed is willing, but the flesh is weak."

MATTHEW 26:41

But without faith it is impossible to please Him,
for he who comes to God must believe that He is,
and that He is a rewarder of those who diligently seek Him.

HEBREWS 11:6

I can do all things through Christ who strengthens me.

PHILIPPIANS 4:13

*I know no blessing so small
      as to be reasonably expected without prayer,
            nor any so great but may be attained by it.*

ROBERT SOUTH

_____

_____

_____

_____

_____

_____

_____

_____

_____

_____

_____

_____

_____

_____

_____

_____

_____

_____

I will go anywhere provided it is forward.

Trust in God and do something.

MARY LYON

Now to Him who is able to do exceedingly
abundantly above all that we ask or think,
according to the power that works in us.

EPHESIANS 3:20

_____

_____

_____

_____

_____

_____

_____

_____

_____

_____

_____

_____

_____

_____

_____

_____

_____

Faith expects from God what is beyond all expectations.

ANDREW MURRAY

I used to ask God to help me.
  Then I asked God if I might help Him.
    I ended up by asking Him to do His work through me.

Every work of God can be traced to some kneeling form.

DWIGHT L. MOODY

By His touch you can experience supernatural
   enthusiasm, boldness, and power.
      It's up to you. Ask every day for the Father's touch.

THE PRAYER OF JABEZ

_____

_____

_____

_____

_____

_____

_____

_____

_____

_____

_____

_____

_____

_____

_____

_____

_____

Be assured, if you walk with God and look to Him
and expect help from Him, He will never fail you.

GEORGE MUELLER

You will show me the path of life;
In Your presence is fullness of joy;
At Your right hand are pleasures forevermore.

PSALM 16:11

_____

_____

_____

_____

_____

_____

_____

_____

_____

_____

_____

_____

_____

_____

_____

_____

_____

_____

God denies a Christian nothing but with
a design to give him something better.

RICHARD CECIL

Bless the LORD, O my soul,
    And forget not all His benefits.

PSALM 103:2

Thou art coming to a King.
    Large petitions with thee bring.
For His grace and power are such that
    None can ever ask too much.

JOHN DONNE

The Lord knows how to deliver the godly out of temptations.

2 PETER 2:9

_____

_____

_____

_____

_____

_____

_____

_____

_____

_____

_____

_____

_____

_____

_____

_____

_____

_____

_____

For with God nothing

will be impossible.

LUKE 1:37